The Witch's Pig

A Cornish Folktale

Adapted by Mary Calhoun
Illustrated by Lady McCrady

William Morrow and Company   New York 1977

Printed in the United States of America.

1   2   3   4   5   6   7   8   9   10

Library of Congress Cataloging in Publication Data

Calhoun, Mary.
   The witch's pig:

   SUMMARY: An adaptation of a Cornish folktale
that tells of the misfortunes that befall a man
who tries to outwit a woman thought to be a witch.
   [1. Folklore—Cornwall. 2. Folklore—England]
I. McCrady, Lady. II. Title.
PZ8.1.C156Wi   [398.2]   [E]   76-27321
ISBN 0-688-22092-4
ISBN 0-688-32092-9 lib. bdg.

Now Betty Trenoweth claimed the power
to heal or ill wish,
and she was known for a witch.
But her cousin Tom said
she was naught but a noddy old woman.
He said she didn't have sense enough
to be a witch.
It happened one day
that Betty saw a fine young pig
at the market in Penzance,
and she determined to buy the pig
to fatten for winter's use.

She began to bargain over the price
with the pig keeper.
Well, Tom was at the market,
and he wanted that pig, too,
but he thought he'd let old Betty
do his work for him.
He watched her haggle the price down,
until she and the seller
were only a few pence apart.

"Thirty pence, and that's a bargain
for a fifty-pence pig," said the pig keeper.
"Twenty-three pence
and not a farthing more!" declared Betty.
She turned away as if she didn't care,
to let the pig keeper think about his lost sale.
He was about to call her back
and offer the pig for twenty-five pence,
when up stepped Tom.
"I'll give you twenty-eight pence," he said,
"and rid you of that haggling old woman."
"Done!" said the pig keeper.

BIGGY BAT
△ △ △
PALMS READ
FORTUNES TOLD

1P

5P

FISH
FRUITERERS

Tom paid over the money
just as Betty came back for her pig.
"Too late, cousin. I've bought the sow."
Tom laughed in Betty's face.

"Why did you interfere,
when I was nearly in price?"
cried the old woman.
"You'll find that sow
the dearest bargain you ever had.
You'll have no use of her!"
Betty shook her bony finger
at Tom and the pig.
"Squonk!" grunted the pig.

Over the hills she led Tom a merry dash,
until he got her home.
He herded the sow into the pigsty
and latched the gate.
"Now stay put!" he said.
"Clever I was, to get you at a bargain price!"

Next morning
the pigsty gate was open,
and the young sow was rooting
in a neighbor's garden.
She snooted up potatoes
with her snout.

She stood on her hind legs
and chewed corn from the stalks.

And when Tom came after her, she ran.

Tom needed half the boys
of Churchtown parish
to herd the troublesome beast
back into her pen again.
The boys said the pig was bewitched,
but Tom said all pigs were contrary.

Yet no matter how Tom barred the gate,
that light-footed pig got out
and scampered through the lanes.
She rooted in many a neighbor's field,
and Tom had to pay
for the mischief she did.

One morning,
when Tom was taking his pig home again,
along came Betty knitting at a stocking,
clicking her needles.

Not a bit like a witch,
friendly as if butter wouldn't melt in her mouth,
she said, "Cousin Tom, I know how
to tame a runaway pig.
Better sell her to me at my price,
twenty-five pence."
"Nay, I'll never sell her to you,
you noddy old woman!"

Feed the sow better, Tom decided.
Then she'd stay home.
For the next month he fed the pig
on corn and meal and milk.
But the more she ate,
the leaner and lankier she became.
And she still ran away.
Tom told of his troubles
at the Bird-in-Hand Inn.
A neighbor said, "That sow has been
ill wished by Witch Betty."
"Ah, her head is as woolly
as her knitting yarn!" Tom declared.
"She's naught but a noddy old woman."

One day Betty leaned over
the pigsty fence,
clicking the needles at her knitting.
Nice as if cheese wouldn't choke her,
she said, "Well, Tom Trenoweth,
are you going to fatten
that pig for Christmas?
Better sell her to me,
though she's no longer worth
twenty-five pence."
"Squonk!" The sow stood up
with her hooves on the fence
and looked at Betty.
"Nay, you've begrudged
that pig to me," Tom cried,
"and I wouldn't sell her to you,
if she didn't fatten in seven years!"

The pig didn't fatten
in the next month, anyway.
Tom saw she had eaten or destroyed
more than she was worth.
To spite old Betty, he decided
to sell the pig at Penzance market.
He put a rope on the pig's leg
and led her down to the stream
in Bojew valley,
where Betty wouldn't see them going.

At the stream, however,
there was no bridge,
and the pig refused to enter the water.
"Squonk!" The sow sat down
on her haunches.
Tom picked up her hind legs and tried
to trundle the pig through the water,
wheelbarrow fashion,
but she dug in her front hooves.

Tom tried to drag her through the water,
but the pig turned
and bolted between his legs. "Squee-onk!"
Tom toppled in the muddy water.
The rope slipped from his hand.

Then the pig led Tom a chase
across the moors,

over hedges and ditches,
"Squonk!"

through bogs and brambles,
"Squee-hee-honk!"

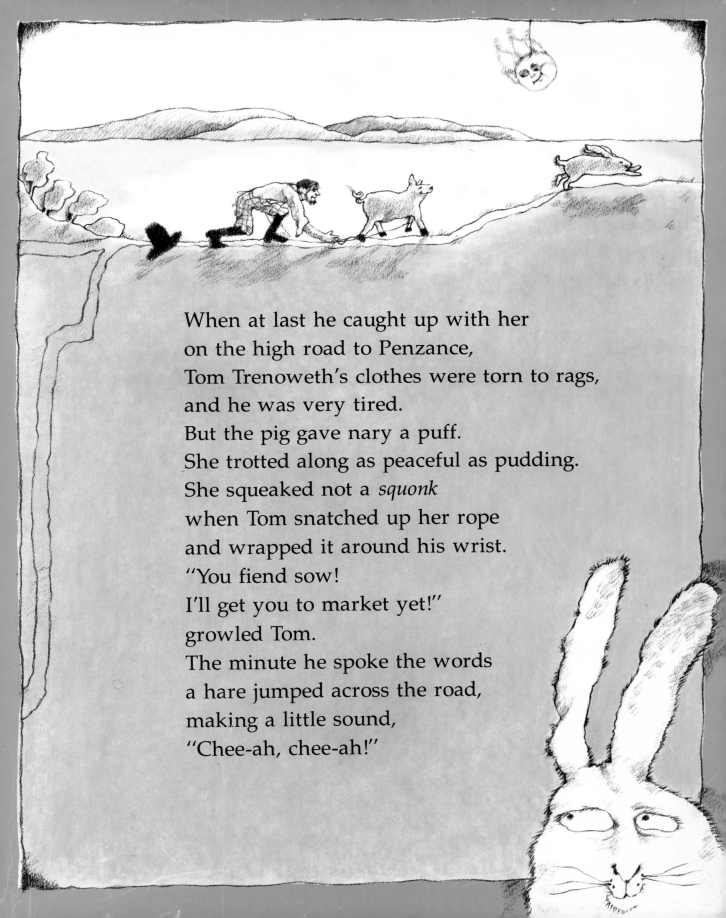

When at last he caught up with her
on the high road to Penzance,
Tom Trenoweth's clothes were torn to rags,
and he was very tired.
But the pig gave nary a puff.
She trotted along as peaceful as pudding.
She squeaked not a *squonk*
when Tom snatched up her rope
and wrapped it around his wrist.
"You fiend sow!
I'll get you to market yet!"
growled Tom.
The minute he spoke the words
a hare jumped across the road,
making a little sound,
"Chee-ah, chee-ah!"

Away raced the pig, after the hare,
down the moor, dragging Tom by the rope.
At the bottom was a road
and a little bridge over a trickle of water
that ran through a drain hole.
The hare darted into the drain,
"chee-ah, chee-ah,"
and the pig dashed after the hare.

Tom's arm was nearly
dragged out of his shoulder,
but he had a knife, so he cut the rope.
The sow scuffled into the drain—
and there she stuck,
with her haunches poking out of the hole.

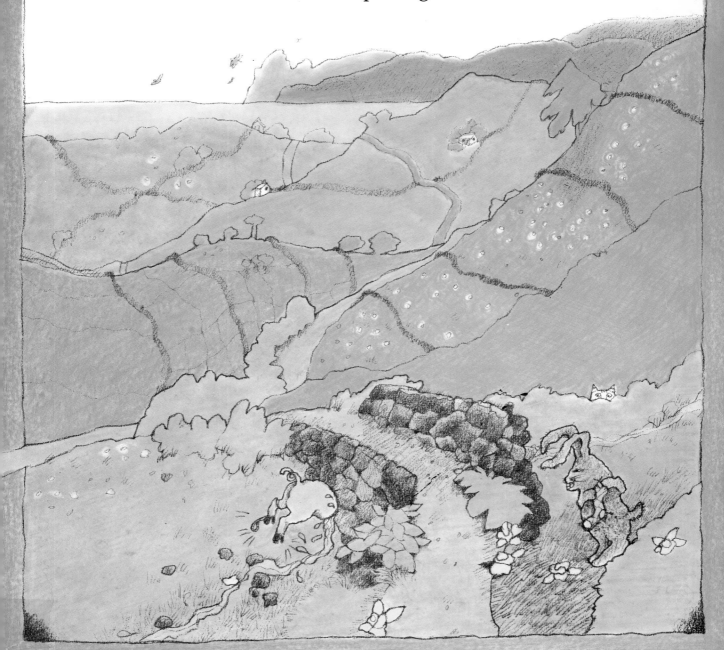

Tom seized her hind legs and hauled.
"Squee-onk!" The pig heaved.
She was stuck like a cork in a bottle,
half in and half out of the hole.
It was past noon, and Tom was very hungry.
Yet he didn't dare leave, for if he did,
the sow might wiggle out somehow
and bolt away.

He went to the other end of the drain
and poked a stick at the pig.
He blathered and coaxed
and threw rocks at the pig.
Skinny she was, and struggle she did,
but the sow couldn't go forth or come back.
"Then stick there!" Tom cried in disgust.
"Bad riddance to you!"

Just then, down the lane came old Betty,
basket on her arm,
needles working at her knitting,
clicketty-clicketty.
"Arrea, cousin, why are you shouting
under the bridge?" she asked,
nice as if butter wouldn't melt in her mouth
or cheese choke her.

"Have you no eyes?" Tom exclaimed.
"Can't you see my pig is in the drain?"
"My pig," said Betty mildly enough.
"Now will you sell her to me?
She's gone to skin and bones,
so she's lost her worth,
but I'll give you ten pence."

Tom thought cleverly,
Let the noddy old woman
find out for herself that the pig
was stuck forevermore in the drain.
"Add to that price
some bread from your basket," he said,
"and you may have her!"
Betty laughed.

"Cousin Tom, you may learn yet
to do your own bargaining. Very well."
She gave him ten pence
and a two-penny loaf from her basket.
Then she called to the pig,
"Chee-ah, chee-ah!"
There was the sound
of squeaking and scuffling.
And the sow backed out of the hole,
slick as a greased pig.
Away she followed old Betty.
Tom sat on the bridge and gnawed his bread.
Sadly he thought, Never again would he call
Betty Trenoweth a noddy old woman,
not she who could take the shape of a hare.
Never again would he cheat a witch
to get a bargain.

As for Betty, she led the pig home, *squonk*.
There she fattened her soon
and kept her for a brood sow.

And many a fat piglet grew up,
child to the witch's pig.

Author's Note

The legends of West Cornwall were passed on and kept alive by droll-tellers, and those semiprofessional storytellers were always welcome to "droll away the time" at firesides, fairs, and feasts. Their stories reflected local beliefs in the magic of fairies, witches, and giants and were characterized by an interest in homely detail and cheerful bits of humor. In the midnineteenth century, folklorist William Bottrell collected and wrote down the old tales in three volumes of *Traditions and Hearthside Stories of West Cornwall.* The story of "The Witch's Pig" is contained in the volume published in 1873 and seems to have been told for nearly one hundred years before that date. Some people believed that certain old women had witchly powers; others scoffed at the idea. However, a number of legends attached themselves to the name of Betty Trenoweth, and this story of her pig is one of them. A motif running through the folklore of Devon and Cornwall is the notion that a magical woman had the power to change into a hare. "Chee-ah" is the traditional way to call a pig.